EXPLORING COUNTRIES
Singapore
I0760246
JOHN PERRITANO
MEDIA ENHANCED BOOKS
AV2
BY WEIGL
ADDED VALUE • AUDIO VISUAL
www.av2books.com

Go to www.av2books.com, and enter this book's unique code.

BOOK CODE

AVB66838

AV² by Weigl brings you media enhanced books that support active learning.

AV² provides enriched content that supplements and complements this book. Weigl's AV² books strive to create inspired learning and engage young minds in a total learning experience.

Your AV² Media Enhanced books come alive with...

Audio
Listen to sections of the book read aloud.

Video
Watch informative video clips.

Embedded Weblinks
Gain additional information for research.

Try This!
Complete activities and hands-on experiments.

Key Words
Study vocabulary, and complete a matching word activity.

Quizzes
Test your knowledge.

Slideshow
View images and captions, and prepare a presentation.

... and much, much more!

Published by AV² by Weigl
350 5th Avenue, 59th Floor
New York, NY 10118
Website: www.av2books.com

Library of Congress Control Number: 2019938429

ISBN 978-1-7911-0894-6 (hardcover)
ISBN 978-1-7911-0895-3 (softcover)
ISBN 978-1-7911-0896-0 (multi-user eBook)
ISBN 978-1-7911-0897-7 (single-user eBook)

Printed in Guangzhou, China
1 2 3 4 5 6 7 8 9 0 23 22 21 20 19

062019
311018

Editor Heather Kissock
Art Director Terry Paulhus
Layout Tammy West

Photo Credits
Every reasonable effort has been made to trace ownership and to obtain permission to reprint copyright material. The publishers would be pleased to have any errors or omissions brought to their attention so that they may be corrected in subsequent printings.

Weigl acknowledges Getty Images, Alamy, Singapore Dance Theatre, Shutterstock, and iStock as its primary photo suppliers for this title.

Contents

Singapore Overview

Singapore, officially named the **Republic** of Singapore, is a wealthy island **city-state** in Southeast Asia. The country's location is the main reason for its prosperity. The island sits at the southern end of the Strait of Malacca, which connects the Indian Ocean with the South China Sea. Ships from around the world use this passage. They often stop at Singapore's deepwater port to receive and deliver goods. This has made the port one of the busiest and largest in the world. Many people have moved to Singapore to take advantage of the country's strong **economy**. As a result, Singapore, with a population of more than 5.5 million, is one of the most densely populated countries on Earth.

The Marina Bay Waterfront hosts some of Singapore's largest celebrations. Many of the city's main attractions are found along its promenade.

Once a common form of transportation for Singapore's locals, trishaws are now used mainly for the tourist trade.

Singapore's Chinese Garden showcases the important role Chinese culture plays in the city.

Singapore's modern outlook can be seen in structures such as the Helix Bridge, a pedestrian walkway that spans the head of the Singapore River.

Receiving guests since 1887, the Raffles Hotel is one of Singapore's oldest and best-known hotels.

Exploring Singapore

Singapore is located at the southern tip of the Malay Peninsula. Malaysia lies to the north, west, and east, and Indonesia to the south. Two **causeways** link the country to the Malay mainland. Singapore covers an area of 255 square miles (660 square kilometers). The main island is diamond-shaped. It is about 26 miles (42 km) from west to east and 14 miles (23 km) from north to south. More than 60 smaller islands surround it.

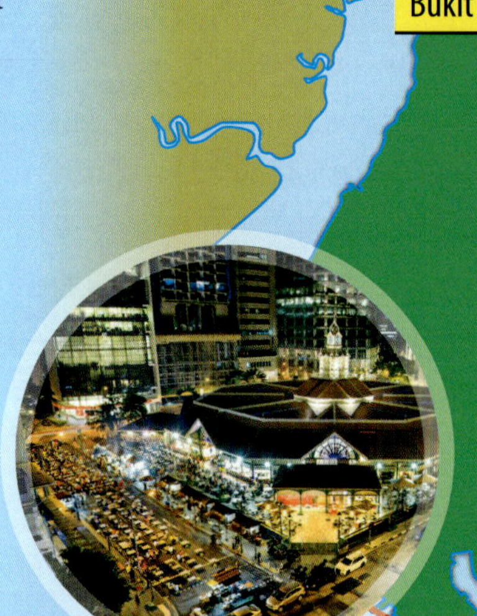

Malaysia

Bukit Timah Hill

City Centre

Sentosa

Map Legend

Singapore

Land

Water

Sentosa

Bukit Timah Hill

Kallang River

City Centre

SCALE

250 Miles

250 Kilometers

Bukit Timah Hill

Standing at 535 feet (163 meters), Bukit Timah Hill is the highest hill in Singapore. It is also one of the few areas of **primary rainforest** on the island. The Bukit Timah Nature Reserve has been created to protect the many animals and plants that live on the hill.

City Centre

Singapore's downtown area stretches along the island's southern coast. The area is known for its shops, **quays**, and towering skyscrapers. Many of the world's best-known companies have offices here.

Sentosa

The island of Sentosa is located off the south coast of Singapore's main island. It has been developed to be a place for people to relax and have fun. The island is home to several beaches, luxury resorts, and an amusement park.

Kallang River

The Kallang River flows from the Lower Peirce Reservoir in central Singapore south to the Nicoll Highway. At a length of 6.21 miles (10 km), it is Singapore's longest river.

LAND AND CLIMATE

Most of Singapore is less than 50 feet (15 m) above sea level. The island is generally flat, with a few rolling hills running through its center. The west and southwest parts of the island feature a series of escarpments, or low ridges.

Singapore has no major rivers or lakes. Instead, a system of streams drains the island. Those that drain northward are ringed by **mangrove** swamps that stretch far inland.

The Singapore River, which flows through the heart of the city, is only 2 miles (3.2 km) long.

The island has little **arable** land. Much of its soil is hardpan **sedimentary** rock, which has been compacted over time. Such hard soil restricts root growth, making it difficult to grow crops. The eastern half of the island is the least fertile area.

Singapore sits near the equator. As a result, the city-state has a tropical climate, marked by high temperatures, excessive **humidity**, and nearly constant precipitation. The average monthly temperature varies from 81° Fahrenheit (27° Celsius) in June to 77°F (25°C) in January.

The seasons are defined by two main **monsoon** periods. The northeast monsoon season, fueled by northerly to northeasterly winds, begins in December and lasts through early March. It tends to be the wettest season, with rainfall totaling more than 10 inches (25 centimeters) each month. The southwest monsoon season, in which the winds blow from the south, begins in June and lasts through September. July is generally the driest month, with less than 7 inches (18 cm) of rain.

From late March to May, the winds are light and variable. However, severe thunderstorms can occur in the afternoon and early evening. Due to the heavy rainfall the island receives, floods are common.

The Sungei Buloh Wetland Reserve, on the northwest part of the island, features 499 acres (202 hectares) of mangrove, mud flats, ponds, and forest.

Land and Climate BY THE NUMBERS

83.8° Singapore's average daily temperature for May, in Fahrenheit. (28.8°C)

167 Average number of days per year that rain falls on the island.

12.5 inches Average amount of rainfall Singapore receives in December. (31.8 cm)

PLANTS AND ANIMALS

For a long time, the entire island of Singapore was a tropical rainforest with mangrove and freshwater swamps. Today, little remains of the island's original vegetation. As more and more people moved to the island, trees and other plants were removed to make room for homes and other buildings. Mangroves, which once were the hallmark of Singapore, have been greatly reduced. Only small mangrove patches now exist in the northern part of Singapore. In the Bukit Timah Nature Reserve, a small tract of tropical evergreen forest also remains.

The loss of vegetation also impacted the animals that lived on the island. Without food or shelter, some **species** disappeared entirely. Today, Singapore is home to an estimated 80 **mammal** species, including the slow loris, lesser mouse deer, and pangolin. Approximately 300 kinds of birds can also be seen in the area. These range from the house swallow to the Javan mynah. Hundreds of species of reptiles, amphibians, and freshwater fish can also be found in the area.

Plants and Animals BY THE NUMBERS

131 Height in feet of tropical hardwoods in the Bukit Timah Nature Reserve. (40 m)

30 Number of amphibian species in Singapore.

18 inches Average height of the lesser mouse deer. (46 cm)

Slow lorises are arboreal animals. This means they spend most of their time in trees. They are mainly active at night.

NATURAL RESOURCES

Even though Singapore is a prosperous country, its wealth does not come from natural resources. Singapore does not have any valuable mineral, fuel, or agricultural resources. In fact, the country has to **import** nearly all of its food. Fresh water is also scarce.

Less than 1 percent of Singapore's land is suitable for farming. Most of this land is used to grow fruit and vegetables. The output from these crops is low, however, and almost all of the produce is sold in the local market. Some land is also used for raising livestock, such as pigs and chickens.

Due to its proximity to the ocean, Singapore has access to significant fish reserves. Most commercial fishing is done offshore in the Indian Ocean. The catch is used mainly for local consumption.

Natural Resources BY THE NUMBERS

10% Estimated portion of Singapore's food that is grown locally.

194 Total number of vegetable, fish, and egg farms in Singapore in 2018.

48.5 pounds
Amount of fish and seafood consumed per Singaporean every year. (22 kilograms)

Singapore has seen a rise in fish farms in recent years. These farms operate in both freshwater and saltwater locations around the island.

TOURISM

Tourism is a major part of Singapore's economy, with more than 18.5 million visitors arriving in 2018. The majority of tourists come from the United States, China, India, Indonesia, and the United Kingdom. These people come to Singapore to experience the island's food, historic sites, and cultural activities.

Tourists often head to the waterfront to see the Merlion fountain. This mythical creature, which combines a lion's head with the body of a fish, is Singapore's national icon.

The City Centre is often the first place people visit. It is a mix of historical buildings and new architecture. Many visitors take a ride on the Singapore Flyer, Asia's largest observation wheel, to take in an elevated view of the island. Orchard Road is Singapore's main shopping street. Besides shopping malls and department stores, it also has numerous restaurants, art galleries, and movie theaters.

The Singapore Flyer began construction in 2005 and opened to its first guests three years later. At its highest point, the view extends 28 miles (45 km).

Singapore has a variety of museums, covering a multitude of interests. The National Museum of Singapore is the largest on the island. It has two main galleries. The Singapore History Gallery takes visitors on a journey through Singapore's history, from the late 1200s to today. The Singapore Living Galleries focus on the island's fashions, films, and photography. The Singapore Art Museum is housed in a former Catholic boys' school. It features contemporary art from Singapore and Southeast Asia.

Nature is an important draw for many tourists. The Gardens by the Bay, which consists of three separate gardens, is a cornucopia of flowers and other plants. The Singapore Botanic Gardens make up one of the island's largest green spaces. People can stroll along the boardwalks to see the more than 300 plant species grown there. One of these plants is the Singapore orchid, the country's national flower. Telok Blangah Hill Park offers visitors the chance to see birds and butterflies in their rainforest **canopy** home.

Tourism BY THE NUMBERS

$20 billion
Approximate amount in U.S. dollars that tourists spent in Singapore in 2018.

541 feet Height of the Singapore Flyer. (165 m)

1887 Year the National Museum of Singapore opened.

One of the highlights of the Gardens by the Bay is its Supertree Grove. Its trees are made from steel and concrete, and range in height from 82 to 164 feet (25 to 50 m).

INDUSTRY

Industry accounts for 26.1 percent of Singapore's gross domestic product (GDP), the amount of goods and services produced by a country. The country's GDP is increasing by about 3 percent each year. Manufacturing accounts for about one fifth of the country's GDP.

A wide variety of goods are manufactured in Singapore. Much of this manufacturing revolves around the **petrochemical** industry. The country imports vast amounts of crude oil, which is then refined and used to create other products, such as plastics and rubber. Electronics manufacturing is another active industry in the country. Singapore's electronics factories make products ranging from batteries to **semiconductors**.

Other industries in Singapore include ship repair and offshore-drilling platform construction. A number of foreign companies have opened up factories and processing facilities. Many of these companies are involved in the production of chemicals.

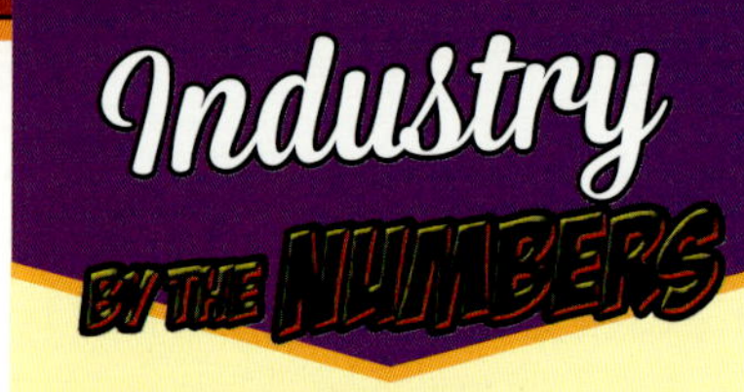

$354 Million
Size of Singapore's GDP in 2018, in U.S. dollars.

13.1% Portion of workers in Singapore with jobs in manufacturing.

No 2 Singapore's rank on the World Bank's 2018 list of best business environments in the world, after New Zealand.

Singapore's electronics manufacturing industry employs about 70,000 people. This number is predicted to increase by 3 percent before 2021.

GOODS AND SERVICES

Seven out of ten Singaporeans are employed in service industries. People in these industries provide services to others rather than produce goods. Teachers, bankers, and store clerks are all service workers. In 2017, Singapore had 196,692 service-related businesses. More than 77,000 of those businesses, or 39.2 percent, were in the wholesale and retail trade. Business services, such as real estate and accounting, made up 23.9 percent of the total number.

Exports are very important to Singapore's economy. The country has the 15th largest export economy in the world. In 2017, it exported more than $320 billion worth of goods. The top exports were electronics, petroleum, and chemical products. Most goods were shipped to Hong Kong, China, and Malaysia.

Singapore also imports many types of goods, spending $293 billion in 2017. Key import products included electronics and other machinery, and crude petroleum. Singapore's main import partners are China, Malaysia, and the United States.

Goods and Services BY THE NUMBERS

More than 200 Number of banks with offices in Singapore.

70.4% Portion the services industry contributed to Singapore's GDP in 2018.

11,500 Approximate number of restaurants in Singapore.

Singapore is home to the world's largest transshipment port. Ships arrive at the port and transfer their containers to other ships. These ships then take the containers to their final destination.

INDIGENOUS PEOPLES

The Malays are the indigenous people of Singapore. Historians believe the Malays originated in Borneo, in the Malay Archipelago. They reportedly **migrated** from Borneo and spread out along the coast of Sumatra and into the Malay Peninsula about 1,500 years ago.

The Orang Laut, a Malay people living mainly along the southern part of the Malay Peninsula, were among the earliest settlers of Singapore. At the time, the island was under the control of the Indonesian city-state of Srivijaya. The Orang Laut were pirates and fishermen. They forced ships sailing between China and India to stop and pay duties, or taxes, to Srivijaya.

It is believed that a prince from Srivijaya, Sang Nila Utama, gave Singapore its name after he saw a lion on its coast. He is said to have founded a city on the site and called it Singapura, which means Lion City. Sang Nila Utama and his **descendants** are believed to have ruled both the city and the island until the 14th century.

Indigenous Peoples BY THE NUMBERS

1299 Year Singapura was founded.

1349 Year Wang Dayuan, a Chinese trader, wrote what is now the only surviving eyewitness account of ancient Singapore.

13.4% Portion of Singapore's current population who are Malay.

Today, the Orang Laut live in coastal villages in Singapore, Malaysia, and Indonesia's Riau Islands.

THE AGE OF EXPLORATION

The Age of Exploration refers to a period between the 15th and 17th centuries. It was a time when European explorers traveled the world's oceans in search of new trade routes to Asia and new sources of wealth for European nations. During the 1500s and lasting through the 1800s, European merchants explored and gained footholds in Southeast Asia.

The Portuguese were the first Europeans to lay claim to land in the region. In 1511, they took control of the city of Malacca. Located on the Strait of Malacca, this city was an important trading port at the time. It was also the capital city of the Malacca sultanate, a kingdom that controlled much of the Malay Peninsula, including Singapore. When the Portuguese invaded Malacca, the sultan fled to Singapore and established a new capital called Johor Lama. The Portuguese destroyed this city in 1587. While Singapore remained part of the Johor sultanate, few people lived on it, and it was largely ignored by the European traders.

The Dutch eventually pushed the Portuguese out of Southeast Asia. They then began establishing their own bases in the area. However, the British, having **colonized** India, also began looking to the east for new lands to add to their growing empire.

The Age of Exploration BY THE NUMBERS

8 Number of sultans who ruled Malacca between 1402 and 1511.

1600 Year English merchants set up the British East India Company to exploit trade in Asia.

1602 Year Dutch traders set up the Dutch East India Company to compete with the British.

Visitors to Malacca, Malaysia, can tour the country's Cultural Museum, located inside a replica of the Sultanate Palace. Inside are prints, photographs, drawings, and artifacts that show the history of the sultanate and the lands it controlled, including Singapore.

EUROPEAN RULE

In early 1819, the British East India Company was looking for a trading site in Indonesia. The company wanted to establish a presence in the area before the Dutch became too dominant. Its representative was a man by the name of Stamford Raffles. He visited several places, but found nothing suitable. This changed, however, on January 29, 1819, when he landed on the island of Singapore.

Raffles's contributions to Singapore went beyond its founding. He also drew up plans for the city, prepared its laws, and founded its first school.

Raffles was amazed by the island's location on the Strait of Malacca. He knew immediately that Singapore was the ideal place for the British East India Company to establish a port. Raffles began negotiations with the Sultan of Johor to establish a trading station on the island.

He soon discovered, however, that the sultan was under the control of the Dutch. Raffles knew that the Dutch would block any British attempt to build on Singapore. He turned to the sultan's brother and began negotiating with him instead. Raffles was successful. Soon after, Singapore became a British settlement.

As more sea traffic came through Singapore, people became aware of the resources the area offered. Rubber and tin became key exports for the port.

In 1824, the Dutch and the British signed a treaty that gave England control of Singapore. Two years later, Singapore and two other British settlements in the region were combined into what was known as the Straits Settlements. By 1867, all three were officially colonies of the British Empire.

With the opening of the **Suez Canal** in Egypt in 1869, ships had a faster route to the Indian Ocean. Trade boomed as a result. The British began expanding Singapore's port, adding more docking areas for ships. They also increased their military presence in the region, building a large naval base on the coast in 1921.

The naval base was not able to protect the island from Japanese invasion during World War II, however. The Japanese had control of Singapore from 1942 until the war ended in 1945. The British then re-established their presence, with Singapore remaining a British colony until 1963. It was at that point that Singapore became part of the Federation of Malaysia. It left the federation after only two years to become an independent nation.

European Rule By the Numbers

14 Age of Stamford Raffles when he began working for the British East India Company.

1832 Year Singapore became the capital of the Straits Settlements.

1 week Time between the Japanese landing on Singapore and the British surrender.

British admiral Louis Mountbatten accepted the final surrender of all Japanese forces in Southeast Asia at Singapore on September 12, 1945. The Japanese High Command had surrendered by order of Emperor Hirohito on August 14.

POPULATION

Singapore is an ethnically diverse nation. Of the 5.6 million people living there, the Chinese make up about three-fourths of the population. They are followed by the Malays and Indians.

With about 47 percent of the population between the ages of 25 and 54, Singapore is a youthful nation. Those 65 and over make up only 13.7 percent. Singaporeans aged 15 to 24 make up nearly 17 percent of the population. The average male can expect to live to be 80.7 years old, while the average female can expect to live to the age of 85.2.

Most Singaporeans live in the southeastern part of the island. However, dense population clusters can be found in the central part as well. Singapore has a population density of 21,712 people per square mile (8,383 per sq. km).

Population BY THE NUMBERS

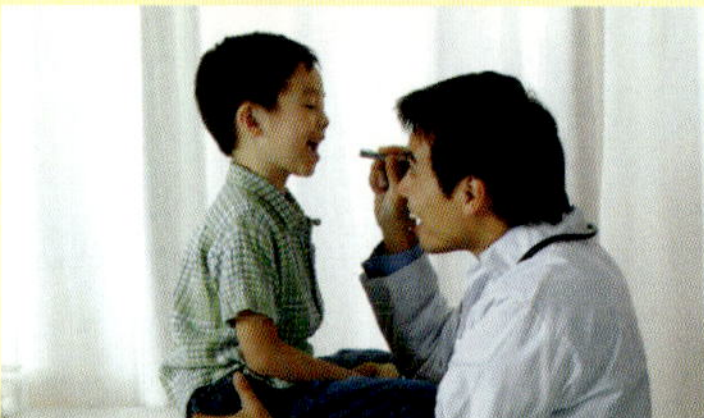

2.2% Portion of the country's GDP spent on public health care.

97 Percentage of those 15 years old and over who can read and write.

40.8 **Median age** of Singapore's population.

In 2019, Singapore's population growth rate was only 1.32 percent, meaning that the population is experiencing very little growth.

POLITICS AND GOVERNMENT

Singapore's government is based on the British **parliamentary** system. There are three separate branches of government. These are the **legislative**, executive, and **judicial** branches. Singapore's parliament is a **unicameral** legislature. Voters elect Members of Parliament (MPs) during regular elections. Each MP serves for a maximum of five years, although new elections can be called at any time.

The head of state is the president. The prime minister is the leader of the government and the leader of the majority party in Parliament. The prime minister is responsible for forming a **cabinet** to help run the government and administer its laws.

Singapore's judiciary is made up of a Supreme Court and State Courts. The Supreme Court is made up of a High Court and a Court of Appeal. The High Court has the power to try all criminal cases. The Court of Appeal hears appeals of all civil and criminal cases. State Courts are made up of District Courts and Magistrate Courts. Both oversee criminal and civil cases.

Politics and Government BY THE NUMBERS

2017 Year Halimah Yacob became Singapore's first female president.

21 Age that Singaporeans are allowed to vote.

6 Number of years that make up the Singaporean president's term in office.

Singapore's Supreme Court building contains 14 civil, 8 criminal, and 3 appeal courts, as well as a cafeteria, library, and gym.

CULTURAL GROUPS

Many people like to visit Kampong Glam's Haji Lane, known for its colorful shops and unique merchandise.

For most of its history, Singapore's people lived in their own **segregated urban** neighborhoods, such as Chinatown for the Chinese, Kampong Glam for the Malays, and Little India for Indians. As times changed and more people moved to Singapore, people began to live in **integrated** neighborhoods. Consequently, these neighborhoods became increasingly diverse in dress, food, and traditions.

The various groups still maintain their culture, but it is with an openness to other influences. Chinese food, for example, is a staple for many people, even those who cannot trace their ancestors back to China. Some dishes now include Indian spices, making them unique to Singaporean culture. Traditional holidays and festivals continue to be celebrated as well. However, the celebrations are not only for one cultural group. All groups are invited to share in the festivities of each culture's celebration.

Chinese New Year is one of Singapore's largest annual celebrations. Crowds flock to the waterfront to watch the spectacular fireworks displays.

In the same way, Singapore is very tolerant of religious freedom. The major religions include Buddhism, Islam, Hinduism, Christianity, and Taoism. Most Singaporeans, approximately 33 percent, are Buddhists, making Buddhism the most practiced religion. The Buddhists are followed in number by Christians, Muslims, and Taoists.

Singapore's rich ethnic landscape even continues into its official languages. English, Mandarin Chinese, Malay, and Tamil are all official languages in Singapore and are listed within the country's **constitution**. However, English is the main language used in commerce, industry, and education. Over time, another language has emerged as well. Singlish is based on English, but contains words from the remaining official languages. It is spoken throughout the island.

Cultural Groups BY THE NUMBERS

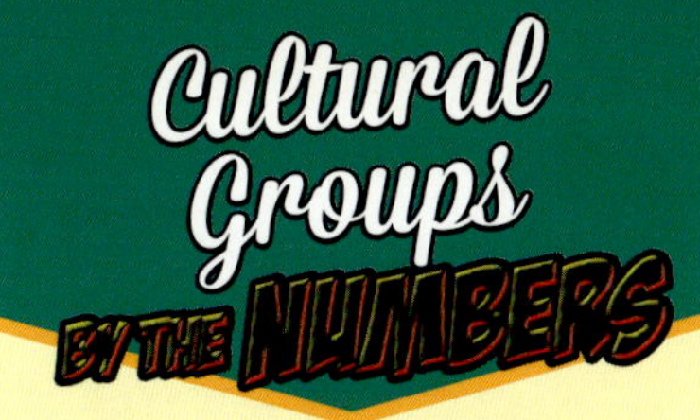

18.7% Portion of Singapore's population that practices Christianity.

2000 Year the first two Singlish words were added to the Oxford online dictionary.

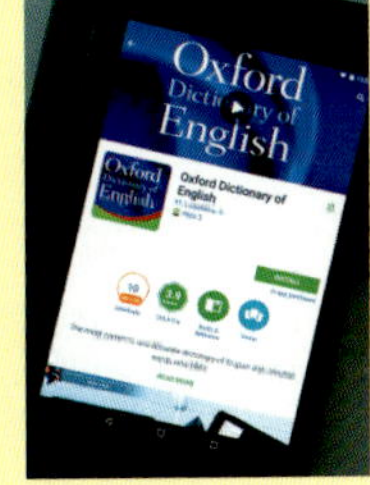

15% Portion of Singaporeans who speak Malay.

The Buddha Tooth Relic Temple is Singapore's best-known Buddhist temple. Besides being a place of worship, it also serves as a meeting place and houses a cafeteria, theater, and museum.

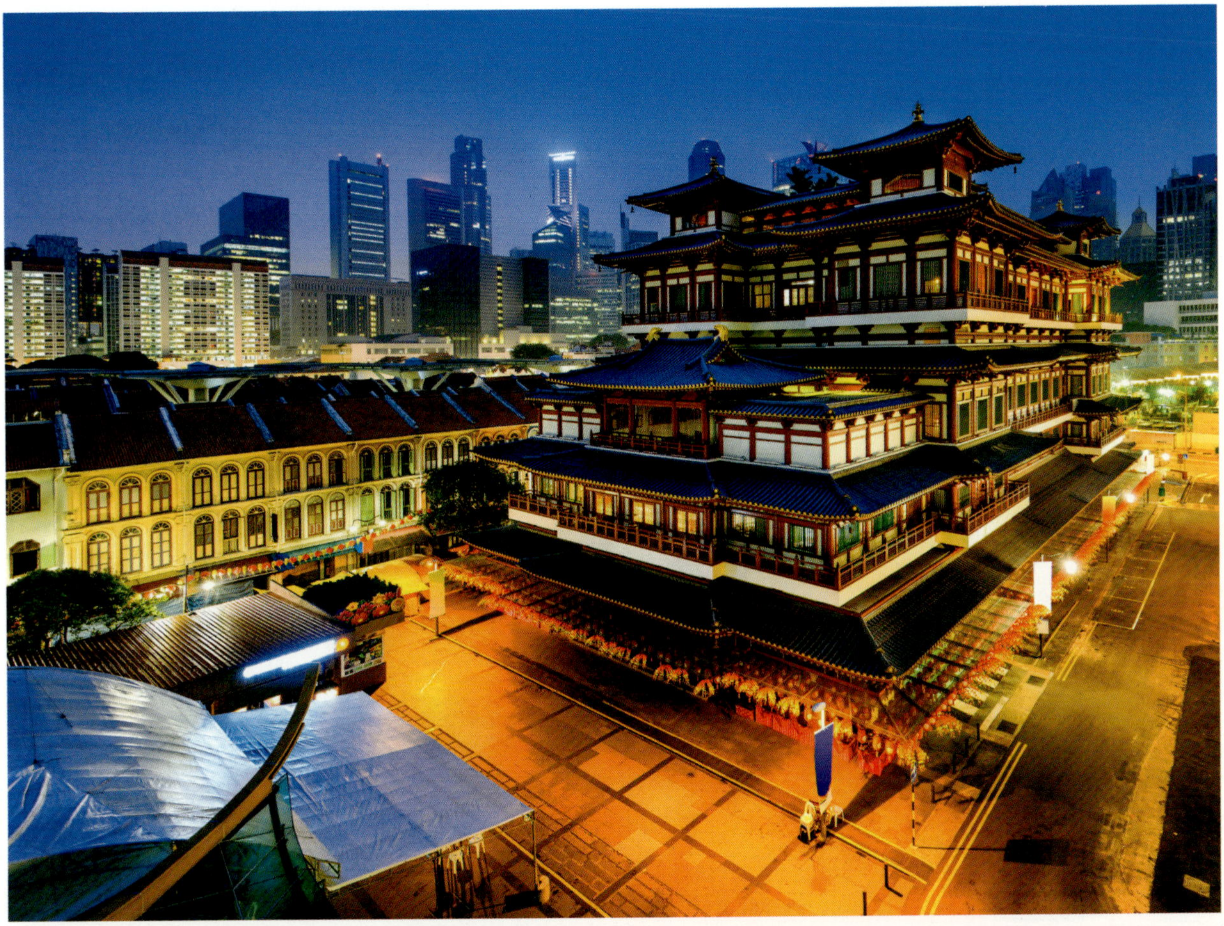

ARTS AND ENTERTAINMENT

Singapore has a wide-ranging arts and entertainment community. It is home to many museums, galleries, shops, and music venues. Millions of dollars have been spent revamping several museums, including the Asian Civilisations Museum and the National Museum of Singapore. Arts festivals, concerts, and vibrant shopping areas also dominate Singapore's arts and entertainment scene.

The Asian Civilisations Museum is the only museum in the region devoted to Asian civilization. It has more than 1,000 artifacts, most dating back at least 5,000 years.

The National Gallery of Singapore holds the largest public collection of modern art in Southeast Asia. The gallery is housed at City Hall and the former Supreme Court. Both are landmarks to the colonial past and Singapore's march toward independence. The gallery has more than 8,000 works, from the 1800s to modern times, including pieces by Singaporean artists Georgette Chen and Liu Kang.

Singapore's ArtScience Museum opened in 2011. Its 21 galleries are spread out over three floors.

The building housing the ArtScience Museum is shaped like a lotus blossom. Its exhibitions combine the natural world and art. One gallery, Future World, is highly interactive and uses cutting-edge technology to focus on art and science.

Singapore also has an active music scene. The St. Jerome's Laneway Festival is one of the country's main music festivals. Spanning two stages, it focuses on indie rock bands and performers. The Singapore International Jazz Festival highlights some of the best jazz performers in the world. Singapore is also home to the Singapore Symphony Orchestra. Founded in 1979, it has performed in concert halls around the world. The Singapore Lyric Opera is one of the few companies in Southeast Asia that performs Western operas.

Singapore has several dance companies. The Singapore Dance Theatre is the country's national ballet company. Founded in 1988, it performs both classical and modern ballets. The Human Expression Dance Company focuses on contemporary works. Every year, it sponsors the M1 CONTACT dance festival, which brings new works to the city's dance community.

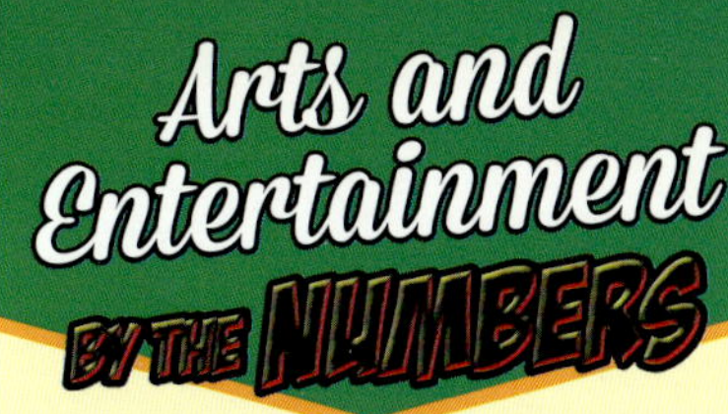

50,000 square feet
Total floor space at the ArtScience Museum. (4,645 sq. m)

45 Number of full-length operas in the Singapore Lyric Opera's repertoire.

2014 Year the first Singapore International Jazz Festival was held.

The Singapore Dance Theatre has embarked on several international tours over the years, performing throughout Asia, as well as in Australia, France, England, and the United States.

SPORTS

Joseph Schooling has continued to impress on the world stage, winning bronze and silver medals at the 2018 FINA Swimming World Cup.

In 2016, Joseph Schooling did something no other athlete from Singapore had ever done. He won an Olympic gold medal. It happened at the Summer Olympics in Rio de Janeiro, when he won the 100-meter butterfly swimming event. While Schooling was the first to win a gold medal, Singapore's first Olympic medal had come years earlier, when Tan Howe Liang won silver in weightlifting in 1960.

From rugby to badminton and table tennis to soccer, sports are extremely popular in this island nation. Soccer, or football as it is called in Singapore, is perhaps the most popular spectator sport. The Singapore Premier League is a professional soccer league made up of nine teams, each with its own stadium. The Singapore national team is one of the best in Southeast Asia. It won the Tiger Cup in 1998 and 2004, the AFF Cup in 2007, and the AFF Suzuki Cup in 2012.

Fandi Ahmed's son, Ikhsan Fandi, has followed in his father's footsteps on the soccer field. He now plays on Singapore's national team.

Many consider Fandi Ahmad to be the best soccer player to come out of Singapore. Born in 1962, Ahmad made a name for himself at the age of 16, when he became the youngest Singaporean to play internationally. He also became the first Singaporean to score a goal in European club competition, when he played for a Dutch club in 1983.

Singapore has never been a world power in sports. However, its athletes have performed well in a variety of table tennis, badminton, bowling, sailing, and swimming competitions. In fact, three of the country's five Olympic medals have been won in table tennis.

One of the first table tennis athletes to see success on the international stage was Jing Junhong. In 2000, she played her way to the Olympic semifinals. She finished fourth in the women's singles event. Four years later, at the Olympics in Athens, Greece, Li Jiawei also finished fourth.

Singaporean players finally made it to the podium in 2008, when Li Jiawei, Feng Tianwei, and Wang Yuegu won Olympic silver in the women's team table tennis event. The three women then won bronze in the same event at the 2012 London Olympics, with Feng Tianwei also winning a bronze in women's singles. All three women were inducted into the Singapore Women's Hall of Fame in 2014.

Sports BY THE NUMBERS

264 Number of athletes representing Singapore at the 2018 Asian Games, the largest contingent the country ever sent.

50.39 seconds Time it took Joseph Schooling to win the gold medal in the 100-meter butterfly in Rio de Janeiro, an Olympic record at the time.

2010 Year the women's national table tennis team defeated the powerhouse China team at the World Table Tennis Championships.

At the 2012 Olympics, Li Jiawei and Wang Yuegu competed against the South Korean team for the bronze medal, winning with a score of 3–0.

Mapping Singapore

We use many tools to interpret maps and to understand the locations of features such as cities, states, lakes, and rivers. The map below has many tools to help interpret information on Singapore.

MAP LEGEND

City Centre	Body of Water	Longitude & Latitude
Town	River	Singapore
Airport	Mountain	Other Countries

N S E W

SCALE

0 10 Miles

0 10 Kilometers

Mapping Tools

- The compass rose shows north, south, east, and west. The points in-between represent northeast, northwest, southeast, and southwest.
- The map scale shows that the distances on a map represent much longer distances in real life. If you measure the distance between objects on a map, you can use the map scale to calculate the actual distance in miles or kilometers between those two points.
- The lines of latitude and longitude are long lines that appear on maps. The lines of latitude run east to west and measure how far north or south of the equator a place is located. The lines of longitude run north to south and measure how far east or west of the Prime Meridian a place is located. A location on a map can be found by using the two numbers where latitude and longitude meet. This number is called a coordinate and is written using degrees and direction. For example, Singapore's City Centre would be found at 1°17′N and 103°51′E on a map.

Map It!

Using the map and the appropriate tools, complete the activities below.

Using the compass rose

1. Which direction is Bukit Timah from Peirce Reservoir?
2. Which direction is Indonesia from Singapore, at their closest points?
3. Which direction would a person travel if he or she wanted to drive to Malaysia from Singapore's City Centre?

Distances between points

4. Using the map scale and a ruler, calculate the approximate length of mainland Singapore's coastline.
5. Using the map scale and a ruler, calculate the approximate distance from the southern tip of Kampong Salabin to the northern tip of Indonesia.
6. Using the map scale and a ruler, calculate the approximate distance between Bukit Timah and Singapore Changi Airport.

ANSWERS 1. Southwest 2. Southeast 3. North 4. 120 miles (193 km) 5. 12 miles (19 km) 6. 18 miles (29 km)

Quiz Time

Test your knowledge of Singapore by answering these questions.

1 Which country borders Singapore to the north?

2 What type of climate is most common in Singapore?

3 How many official languages does Singapore have?

4 Which ethnic group dominates Singapore?

5 Which European nation was the first to colonize Singapore?

6 How many branches of government does Singapore have?

7 How much of Singapore's land is suitable for farming?

8 At what age are Singaporeans allowed to vote?

9 Which group of people are indigenous to Singapore?

10 Who was the first Singaporean to win an Olympic gold medal?

ANSWERS

1. Malaysia
2. Tropical
3. Four
4. Chinese
5. England
6. Three
7. Less than 1 percent
8. 21
9. The Malay
10. Joseph Schooling

Key Words

arable: suitable for growing crops

cabinet: group of senior ministers responsible for enacting government policy

canopy: a rooflike covering of leaves and branches that the Sun does not shine through

causeways: raised roads across the water

city-state: a city that is also an independent country

colonized: sent a group of settlers to a new territory to establish political control over it

constitution: the basic laws and principles of a nation

descendants: people who are related to someone who lived in the past

economy: the wealth and resources of a country in which goods and services are produced and consumed

exports: goods sold and sent to other countries

humidity: amount of water vapor in the atmosphere

import: to buy goods from other countries

integrated: a combination of different elements to provide a more agreeable way of life

judicial: relating to the court system

legislative: having the power to make laws

mammal: an animal that has hair or fur and drinks milk from its mother

mangrove: a tropical tree or shrub that grows in swampy areas

median age: the age that half the people in a population are younger than and half are older than

migrated: moved from one area to another

monsoon: the season of heavy rain in some Asian countries

parliamentary: relating to a system of government that has elected members who make the laws for the country

petrochemical: chemical products derived from petroleum

primary rainforest: a tropical forest that exists in its original condition

quays: platforms constructed beside water

republic: a form of government in which the head of state is elected

sedimentary: relating to rock that has been made from mineral and organic fragments

segregated: isolated or set apart from each other

semiconductors: chemical substances used in electronics

species: groups of animals or plants with common characteristics

Suez Canal: a waterway in Egypt that connects the Mediterranean Sea to the Red Sea

unicameral: having a single legislative chamber

urban: relating to city life

Index

Log on to www.av2books.com

AV² by Weigl brings you media enhanced books that support active learning. Go to www.av2books.com, and enter the special code found on page 2 of this book. You will gain access to enriched and enhanced content that supplements and complements this book. Content includes video, audio, weblinks, quizzes, a slideshow, and activities.

AV² Online Navigation

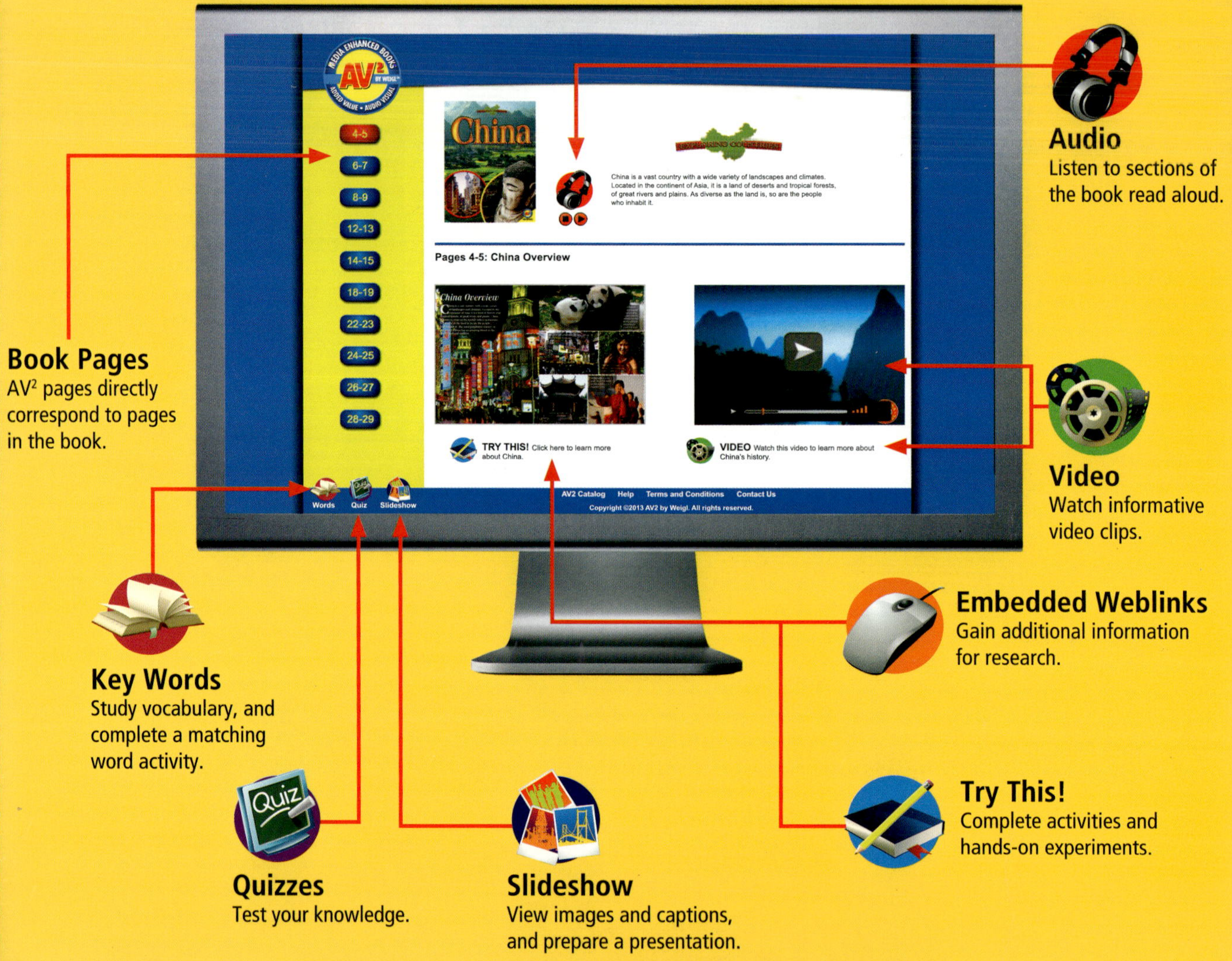

Audio
Listen to sections of the book read aloud.

Book Pages
AV² pages directly correspond to pages in the book.

Video
Watch informative video clips.

Embedded Weblinks
Gain additional information for research.

Key Words
Study vocabulary, and complete a matching word activity.

Try This!
Complete activities and hands-on experiments.

Quizzes
Test your knowledge.

Slideshow
View images and captions, and prepare a presentation.

AV² was built to bridge the gap between print and digital. We encourage you to tell us what you like and what you want to see in the future.

Sign up to be an AV² Ambassador at www.av2books.com/ambassador.

Due to the dynamic nature of the internet, some of the URLs and activities provided as part of AV² by Weigl may have changed or ceased to exist. AV² by Weigl accepts no responsibility for any such changes. All media enhanced books are regularly monitored to update addresses and sites in a timely manner. Contact AV² by Weigl at 1-866-649-3445 or av2books@weigl.com with any questions, comments, or feedback.